INFORMATION LIBRARY

PREHISTORIC LIFE

Theodore Rowland-Entwistle

Gareth Stevens Children's Books
MILWAUKEE

For a free color catalog describing Gareth Stevens' list of high-quality children's books, call 1-800-341-3569 (USA) or 1-800-461-9120 (Canada).

Library of Congress Cataloging-in-Publication Data
Rowland-Entwistle, Theodore.
    Prehistoric life / by Theodore Rowland-Entwistle.
        p.   cm. — (Gareth Stevens information library)
    Bibliography: p.
    Includes index.
    Summary: Describes the characteristics of a variety of
prehistoric life forms from the simplest to the most complex
with emphasis on reptiles and humans.
    ISBN 0-8368-0006-0
    1. Paleontology—Juvenile literature. [1. Paleontology.] I. Title. II. Series.
QE714.5.R69   1989
560—dc20   89-11373

North American edition first published in 1990 by
Gareth Stevens Children's Books
RiverCenter Building, Suite 201
1555 North RiverCenter Drive
Milwaukee, Wisconsin 53212, USA

Photographic credits: Ann Ronan Picture Library 12 (left), 13; Bridgeman
Art Library 9 (top), 11 (top); ET Archive 10; Geoscience Features 15, 20, 28;
Michael Holford 8, 9; Natural Science Photos 5, 11 (bottom), 14, 17, 19, 23
(bottom), 24 (left), 29, 34, 35 (bottom), 37 (bottom), 41, 48, 51, 56, 57 (right);
NHPA 23 (top), 31, 37 (top), 48 (bottom); Nigel Press 7; Oxford Scientific Films
8, 12 (top and bottom right), 33, 42, 44; Planet Earth 24 (right), 26, 30, 32, 35
(top); Robert Harding Picture Library 18, 47

Illustrated by David Holmes and Eugene Fleury

Series editors: Neil Champion, Mark Sachner, and Rita Reitci
Research editor: Scott Enk
Educational consultant: Dr. Alistair Ross
Editorial consultant: Neil Morris
Design: Groom and Pickerill
Cover design: Kate Kriege
Picture research and art editing: Ann Usborne
Specialist consultant: Dr. Gwynne Vevers

Printed in the United States of America

1 2 3 4 5 6 7 8 9 96 95 94 93 92 91 90

Contents

1: PLANTS AND ANIMALS

Living Things Today

The world around us teems with living things. Some are plants, which cannot move around. Some are animals, most of which are able to move. Many more are microorganisms — tiny simple living things that are neither plants nor animals. They include bacteria and the living organisms called algae that often form green slime on ponds.

There are about 350,000 different known kinds of plants and over a million kinds of animals. We call each different kind of living thing a species. Biologists classify all these species to identify them and show how they are related. Swedish naturalist Carolus Linnaeus worked out the system in 1735.

Each species receives a Latin name. We use Latin names because many plants and animals have no common names. One species may have many common names.

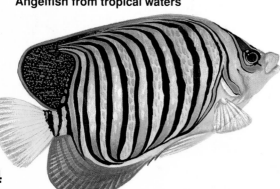

Hummingbird from North and South America

Spotted souslik, a European ground squirrel
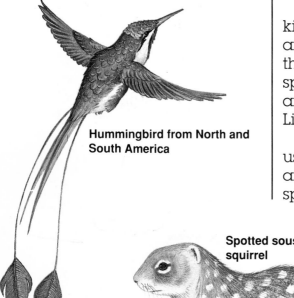

Starfish from coastal waters

Angelfish from tropical waters
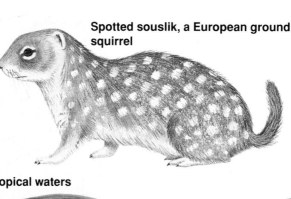

Arrow-poison frog from South America

Many others have the same common name. For example, "robin" is the common name for eight different species of birds.

Living things of yesterday

For every species of plant and animal alive today there were ninety-nine more that lived in prehistoric times and are now extinct — that is, they have died out. One reason for this is that new species took their places. The process of forming new species is known as evolution. Evolution has been going on for millions of years. The earliest known living things of the past were some bacteria whose remains have been found to be about 3.5 billion years old.

Evolution is still going on, but the process is so slow that we hardly notice it. Some species have become extinct fairly recently — often because of human interference in the natural world. The mammoth died out only 10,000 years ago. The dodo, a flightless bird, died out in 1681. The passenger pigeon died out in 1914. Many other species are in danger, including the giant panda, the Bengal tiger, the orangutan, the river terrapin, the far northern flax snail, and the Chiapas slipper orchid.

▲ The orangutan of Sumatra and Borneo is an endangered species. Only about 5,000 are still alive.

Classification

Classification consists of a series of ranks:

Kingdom: There are five of these large groups, one for animals, one for plants, and three for other organisms, such as fungi, bacteria, and amoebas.

Phylum (*plural:* phyla): All organisms of the same basic type are grouped in a phylum. Example: chordates (animals with backbones, including fish, birds, and mammals). For plants, the word "division" sometimes replaces "phylum."

Class: A more closely related group. Example: the mammals, such as cats, whales, and cows.

Order: A subdivision of a class. Example: the carnivores (animals that eat flesh) such as cats, wolves, and dogs.

Family: A subdivision of an order. Example: the cat family.

Genus: A subdivision of a family. Example: the big cats, such as lions and tigers.

Species: Animals that really are alike. Every single lion alive is from the same species.

Mushroom, or fungus   **Plant-eating bug**

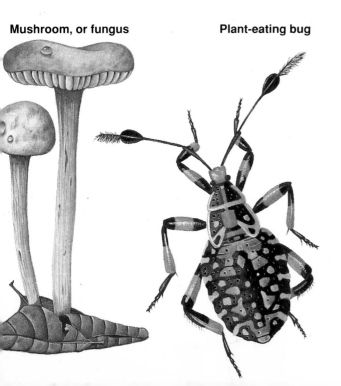

Earth: A Living Planet

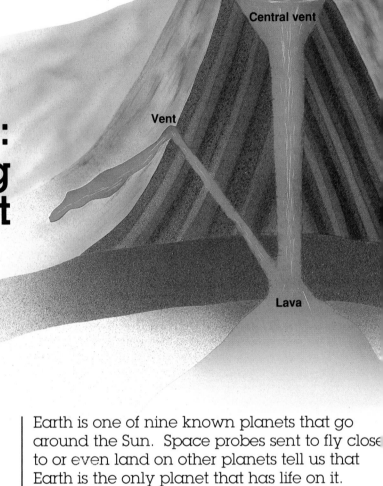

Crater

Central vent

Vent

Lava

A volcano builds a cone of ash ▶ and lava around its central vent, where a crater forms. Another vent may open in the side of the cone.

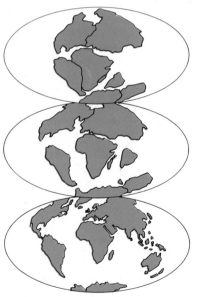

▲ The top map shows the continents as they were about 140 million years ago, about 60 million years after they began separating. The other maps show how they moved to their present positions (bottom).

Earth is one of nine known planets that go around the Sun. Space probes sent to fly close to or even land on other planets tell us that Earth is the only planet that has life on it. Earth itself also seems to be "alive" because it changes all the time. The rock deep inside Earth is so hot that it is molten. Volcanoes brin this molten rock to the surface. Earthquakes shake some regions, like Japan, Iceland, and parts of the west coast of the Americas.

Oceans and large lakes, stirred by winds and currents, keep moving. Both rain and win wear away the land in a process called erosic Rivers carry sand and mud from the land into the ocean.

Continents divide

We can see many changes taking place. But many more take place so slowly that we do not notice them. More than 200 million years ago, the west coast of Africa and the east coa

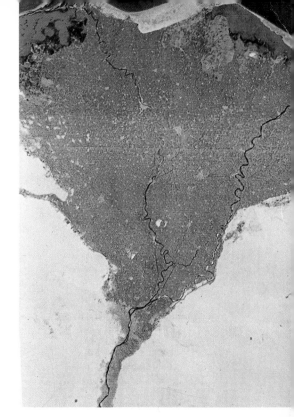

▲ A picture from a satellite showing the delta of the Nile River, built up over centuries by silt washed down the river. The computer-enhanced coloring shows the area where plants are able to grow.

of South America fit next to one another. They were part of a supercontinent that we now call Gondwanaland. This landmass also included what is now Australia, India, and Antarctica. Gondwanaland broke up, and the continents began to drift apart. They are still drifting. Earth's surface is covered by large tectonic plates on which the continents sit. When two plates meet, one slides under the other, sinking down inside the Earth. The plate on top moves upward, raising mountains. The Rockies, the Andes, and the Alps all rose in this way.

Another slow change involves the level of the sea. A great deal of water is frozen and held in the ice caps that cover the North and South poles. Those ice caps may vary in size. When they are large, the level of the sea is lower and this exposes more land. When the ice melts, the water running into the oceans raises the sea level. Then the sea floods the low-lying land.

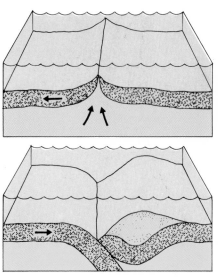

▲ The process of seafloor spreading. Top: New material wells up from volcanoes along the midocean ridges, forcing the plates apart. Bottom: One plate sinks under another.

7

Stories of Creation

Most scientists today believe that all living things have evolved over millions of years. However, some people think that living things were created in their present form by God, or by many gods. People have always been curious about the origin of life and the world that we live in. They based their ideas on what they saw and believed to be true. For example, we know that Earth goes around the Sun. But at one time people knew only that the Sun seemed to move across the sky while Earth stayed still. Earth is round, but when people knew only a small part of the world, they thought Earth was flat. When the huge bones of prehistoric animals were first discovered, about three hundred years ago, many people believed that they were the bones of giant humans.

Some creation legends

The Hebrew writers of the Book of Genesis said that their God created the heavens and Earth out of a vast ocean. Hundreds of years earlier the people of Mesopotamia, now part of Iraq, believed that Earth and humans were created as a result of a war between the gods.

Some American Indian creation legends also told of a vast sea. A divine crab, fish, or tortoise

▲ Evidence of ancient life is found in rocks. These bones at Dinosaur National Monument, in Utah, belonged to a dinosaur that lived between 225 million and 65 million years ago.

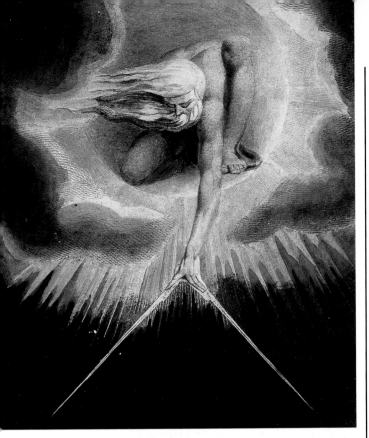

created land out of mud from the sea. Some Pacific islanders thought that at first there was a great emptiness, from which the world slowly came into being. The ancient Norse legends also spoke of a great emptiness, from which came the first living thing, a giant named Ymir. The god Odin killed Ymir and formed the land and sea out of the giant's body.

Darwin's Theory

HMS *Beagle*, the ship in which Charles Darwin sailed for five years in the 1830s, anchored in a bay off Tierra del Fuego. Darwin's discoveries led to the theory of evolution by changes he called natural selection. ▼

In December 1831, a 22-year-old naturalist set off on a great adventure. Charles Darwin had been invited to join a scientific voyage around the world. He sailed in a small warship, HMS *Beagle*. The voyage lasted nearly five years. During that time, young Darwin studied the plants, animals, and geology of South America, Australia, New Zealand, and the Pacific island

Darwin never traveled again, but in those five years he had gathered enough informatic to help him form his theories of evolution. One thing that struck him was the great variety of different species he had seen. Where had they all come from? Some other scientists were wondering about that, too, but none of them had found a good answer up to that time.

Darwin was particularly interested in a group of birds called finches. He found them in the Pacific Ocean, on the Galápagos Islands off the coast of Ecuador in South America. For this reason we now call these birds Darwin's finches. These finches are so alike that they

◀ Charles Darwin was 50 years old when this picture of him was painted. At that time, he was completing his theory of evolution.

are obviously related. Yet they have differently shaped beaks to help them eat different kinds of foods. Some, for example, eat seeds, while others eat insects.

Twenty years of thought

Darwin thought that these finches must all be descended from just one kind of finch. He thought about their differences for nearly twenty years. He noticed that farmers could breed different kinds of cows, some to produce good meat, others to give rich milk. It seemed that just as the farmers could change the cows, natural processes could change the finches. He called the process of change natural selection. For example, some species of finches had developed a short, strong bill, just right for cracking the hard seeds they ate.

Darwin's theories are still the basis for our ideas of evolution, and they help explain how life developed in prehistoric times.

Over the centuries, farmers have bred many different kinds of cows from original stock. Top: one of the wild white cattle of Chillingham that are thought to be like the original stock. Bottom: a Jersey cow. ▼

◀ The medium ground finch, one of Darwin's finches from the Galápagos Islands, has a short beak suitable for eating seeds. Some of Darwin's finches have long, slender beaks.

11

Searching for the Past

Scientists today are constantly learning more about prehistoric life and evolution. They are finding many remains of past life preserved in rocks and have discovered how to calculate the age of those rocks and remains.

Present-day research into evolution uses the science of genetics. The theories behind genetics were first set forth by Gregor Mendel, an Austrian monk. Mendel experimented by breeding together short and tall varieties of peas. He found that some of the resulting plants were tall and others short.

Other scientists following up Mendel's work found that features such as height, skin, and hair and eye color are determined by parts of the cells that carry the traits of the animal or plant body. These parts are called genes.

These two pictures show the two colors of the peppered moth. In the upper picture, the normal light moth is harder to see on a clean tree than the dark one. In the lower picture, the light moth shows up clearly against sooty bark, and the dark moth does not.

▲ Gregor Mendel spent his life in the monastery at Brno, Czechoslovakia, and eventually became its abbot.

Mendelian inheritance of color in peas is shown here. On the left are white flowered peas, and on the right, pink ones. In the middle is a flower of a cross between the two, containing mixed coloring.

Leaps and bounds

Darwin thought that changes were gradual and slowly produced different species. Many scientists now think that while gradual changes are in fact going on all the time, there are also sudden jumps in evolution.

An example of gradual evolution is shown by two varieties of an insect, the peppered moth. In the clean air of the countryside, the peppered moth is light in color, and when it rests against the bark of light-colored trees, it is almost invisible to hungry birds. But in towns where the air is sooty, the bark of trees is black. There, a dark variety of the peppered moth thrives, because against the sooty tree bark, it also is hard to see.

Survival

Some people make the mistake of supposing that changes, such as that of the peppered moth, take place so an organism can survive. In fact, the moth survives because it has changed and so matches its new background.

In the same way, birds learn not to eat poisonous wasps, so the wasps survive. Syrphid flies also survive because their black-and-yellow colors make them look like wasps. We call this protective coloration.

Protective coloration: The mountain king snake, on the left, is harmless, but other animals avoid it because it looks like the highly poisonous coral snake, on the right. ▼

2: CLUES TO THE PAST

Reading the Story

Rock strata laid down over many years, in a wall of the Grand Canyon in Arizona. ▶

The rocks that make up Earth's crust — its outer layer — also preserve some of its past. With care and skill we can read a large part of that story in the rocks. There are three basic kinds of rocks. Some have come welling up from inside Earth, all hot and molten. They are called igneous rocks. Others are made up of tiny fragments of rock, like sand, that have come together in layers. The layers have hardened to form fresh rocks. They are called sedimentary rocks because they have formed from sediments. The third kind of rock forms when existing rocks, igneous or sedimentary, change from heat, pressure, and chemical action deep inside Earth. These rocks are called metamorphic rocks.

Glomar Challenger

From 1968 to 1983, a special drilling ship, the *Glomar Challenger*, took cores from the seabed, deep under the oceans. These cores have told us a lot about Earth's history and have also helped us in the search for oil.

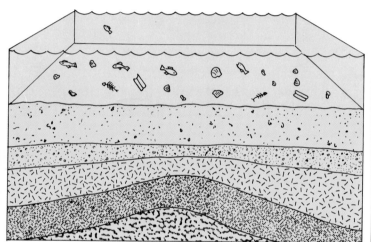

Here you can see different layers of rock laid down at different times over millions of years. They often contain fossils.

◀ Deposits of oil and natural gas can become trapped under layers of rock. Here a layer of waterproof clay keeps oil from leaking upward from a porous layer of rock that has been lifted and folded. Oil forms from the bodies of tiny prehistoric sea animals.

Layers of rock

Sedimentary rocks make up much of our rock "book." These rocks, formed over millions of years, are laid down in layers called strata.

Usually the top layer is the newest and the bottom layer is the oldest. But sometimes great movements of Earth's crust over a long time can fold these rocks so that they lie at an angle, on edge, or even turn upside down with older layers on top of newer ones.

Many sedimentary rocks contain the remains of animals and plants that lived when the rocks were being laid down. Chalk is a kind of rock consisting almost entirely of shells of very tiny sea creatures that lived over 65 million years ago in the Cretaceous period.

▲ Drill cores from samples deep in the ground, lying in long channels called coffins.

Fossils

We know about prehistoric life because the remains of many plants and animals have been preserved as fossils, usually in sedimentary rocks. Some fossils are only a few thousand years old, but others formed many millions of years ago.

Most fossils form when the remains of an animal or plant become buried in sand or silt, usually in watery places such as swamps or riverbeds, or in shallow seas close to the shore. Over a long time, more silt piles on top and becomes stone.

Fossil formation

Fossils can form in four basic ways. Some have turned to stone, some are molds or casts, some are traces, and a few are the actual remains of whole animals or plants.

Stone fossils come about in several ways. A dead animal's bones or shell may become filled with minerals from the water into which it sank. The minerals harden to form stone. The bones

This is how layers of fossils are found in Earth's crust. The time scale has been condensed. In reality, the layers would not be so close together. By matching up fossils found in different places around the world, geologists can tell in which period the animals or plants lived. ▼

or shells survive, reinforced with this stone. Water may dissolve away the body of a plant or animal, and minerals replace it. Then we have a stone replica of the original. Or the soft parts of plants or animals decay, leaving a carbon residue as a print of the original plant or animal in the stone. Often a print is found only when the stone is split.

Sometimes the dead animal or plant just dissolves away, leaving a hollow-mold fossil. This may fill with minerals to form a stone cast of the original organism.

A trace fossil is a mark left by a long-dead creature. Typical trace fossils are footprints left in mud that has since hardened. Often it is difficult to decide which animal made the traces.

Very rarely do we find a whole animal or plant preserved. Occasionally we find insects or other small creatures preserved in amber. Amber is fossilized resin, the clear sticky stuff that oozes from the bark of some coniferous trees.

▲ This fossil fish lived in the Cretaceous period, 140 million to 65 million years ago.

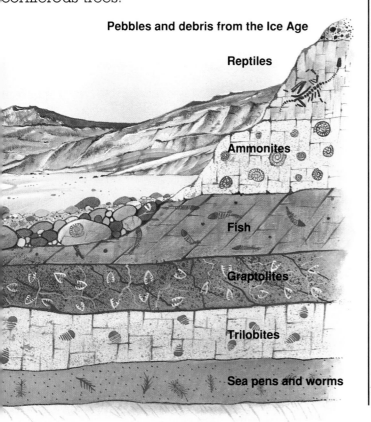

Pebbles and debris from the Ice Age

Reptiles

Ammonites

Fish

Graptolites

Trilobites

Sea pens and worms

Living fossils

- The coelacanth, a primitive fish thought to be extinct for 65 million years, was found alive off South Africa in 1938.

- The ginkgo, a tree native to China and Japan, is the only survivor of a group of plants from 200 million years ago.

- Horsetails are primitive plants that have changed little in 300 million years.

- Neopilina, a mollusk first known from fossils 350 million years old, was found alive in the Pacific Ocean in 1952.

- The tuatara is a lizard living on islands off New Zealand. It is the sole survivor of a group of reptiles that was common about 200 million years ago.

- The Virginia opossum has hardly changed at all in the past 36 million years.

Finding Fossils

You can find fossils almost anywhere there are exposed sedimentary rocks, such as in cliffs near the sea or rivers and in the walls of quarries. Fossils also appear in coal mines. In fact, coal itself is a fossil. It formed from the remains of forests that grew in the Carboniferous period.

Just collecting fossils does not reveal all they have to tell us. The finder must take notes of exactly where and in what layer of rock they were found. This is the only way to read and record the full story of the rock and its fossils.

Fossil logs, 200 million years old, ▶ lie on the desert floor in Petrified Forest National Park, Arizona. Their wood has turned to stone. Fossil trees exist in many parts of the world.

Famous fossil sites

- Fossil remains of dinosaurs are plentiful at Dinosaur National Monument, on the Utah-Colorado border.

- Fossil trees can be seen in the Glasgow Museum in Scotland.

- Neanderthal, or Neander Valley, near Düsseldorf, West Germany, is the site where the first skull of Neanderthal Man was found.

- Olduvai Gorge, Tanzania, contains many fossil remains of early humans, some of them around two million years old.

- Rancho La Brea, near Los Angeles, is the site of tar pits where thousands of animals were trapped in pools of tar during the Pleistocene period over two million years ago.

◀ Collecting fossils can be a time-consuming task requiring a great deal of patience. Here, a collector is brushing dirt from a fossil ichthyosaur — a marine reptile with a body like a porpoise. Next, he will number the bones to identify them.

A matter of life or death

Fossil hunters must also record any other fossils found nearby. For example, an assortment of animal bones near human skeletons may show what our distant ancestors ate. Sometimes fossils are found in the place where the plants or animals once lived. A group of fossils found together like this is called a life assemblage. But often you find a pile of fossils, especially fossil shells. This kind of pile usually formed when the sea or a river washed the shells together after the animals were dead, just as you find empty shells on the beach today. Such a group is called a death assemblage.

Beware!

Fossil hunting can be dangerous, so you should be sure that an experienced adult goes with you. When near cliffs and in quarries, always wear a hard hat for protection against falling rocks. Along the seashore, watch out for incoming tides that can trap you.

Dating rocks

Radioactivity is one way geologists calculate the age of rocks. Many rocks contain elements such as uranium, thorium, and potassium. These elements slowly change into other elements as they give off radioactivity. Their very slow speed of change, or decay, has been measured. Scientists know how much radioactivity there should be in new rocks. So by measuring how much radioactivity is left in old rocks, they can figure their age.

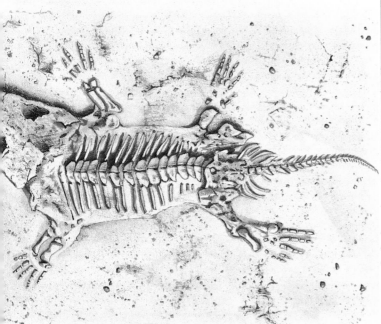

◀ Finding the fossil remains of long-dead animals can be very exciting, especially when they are complete.

Rebuilding Fossils

Iguanodon

A fossil may be completely misleading. For example, a cone-shaped bone of the dinosaur Iguanodon was found in the early 1800s. People thought it was a horn like that of a rhinoceros. Then, in 1878, a patch of sand full of huge bones was found in a Belgian coal mine. More than 30 complete Iguanodon skeletons were dug out and reassembled. The "horn" turned out to be the animal's thumb bone!

A painting showing plants and animals of the Cretaceous period, 65-140 million years ago. The animals include dinosaurs and pterosaurs — flying reptiles with wings of skin, like bats, more than 16 feet (5 m) across. ▶

Finding and excavating a fossil is only part of the story. It takes great skill and knowledge to put a collection of scattered bones back together to build up a skeleton. Some early attempts to reconstruct dinosaurs were completely wrong. That was because no complete skeletons had been found at the time. The scientists had to guess what the missing parts were and how the bones had fit together in life to form an animal they had never seen.

A lot depends on how carefully the fossils are dug out. Accurate notes, photographs, and drawings must be made to show how the bones were lying when found.

Often males and females of the same species are of different sizes. Male elephants are larger than females, and female spiders are larger than males. Similar differences have sometimes misled scientists into thinking they had found fossils of two separate species.

Cleaning and repairing

Rebuilding a fossil skeleton may take months of work in a laboratory. Workers clean the bones and put broken bones together, often

reinforcing them with steel rods. If some bones are missing, they may make fiberglass or plaster copies of similar bones. For example, if the bones of only one foreleg are found, those of the other foreleg will normally be mirror images of the ones found.

Sometimes it is possible to make a lifelike model of a prehistoric animal. Scientists who study anatomy — the structure of animals — know what muscles are likely to fit on a skeleton. But the skin may be a matter of guesswork. The great cave bear, for instance, probably had skin and fur much like those of modern bears. Extinct reptiles are likely to have had skin similar to that of modern reptiles.

The skeletons displayed in museums of prehistoric animals like the Iguanodon (left) and the crocodilian (right) are reconstructed. Putting a fossil skeleton together is like doing a three-dimensional jigsaw puzzle, often with some pieces missing. ▼

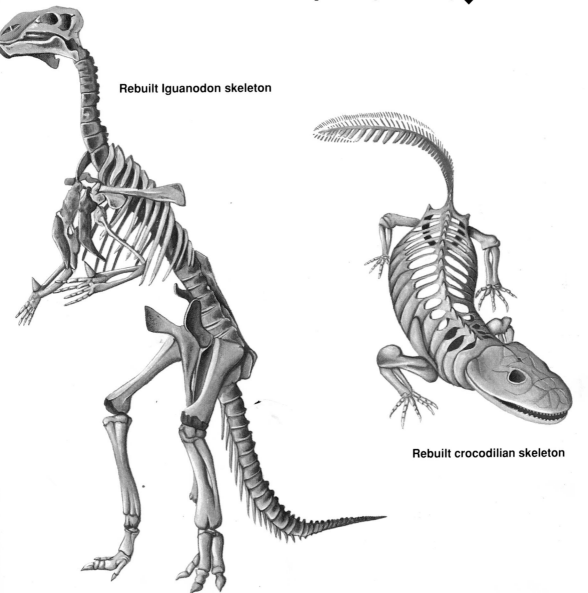

Rebuilt Iguanodon skeleton

Rebuilt crocodilian skeleton

21

3: LIFE IN THE OCEANS

The Early Days

The oldest known rocks are near Granite Falls, Minnesota. They are estimated to be 3.8 billion years old. Earth is about 4.6 billion years old. What happened in those first 800 million years? We have been able to figure out the likely course of events from clues left in Earth's rocks, and from what is happening today.

In its early days, our Earth had a great many volcanoes. These volcanoes hurled out lava and rock. They also expelled great quantities of steam and other gases. The steam slowly turned into water to form the oceans, probably just over four billion years ago.

The other gases released by the volcanoes included many of the gases that we find in the atmosphere today. At first, the atmosphere had very little oxygen, a gas that is essential for life on Earth. Most of the oxygen that Earth had at that time had combined with hydrogen

In its early days, Earth had many volcanoes that erupted clouds of steam and gases. As they do today, violent thunderstorms often accompanied these erupting volcanoes. The steam from the volcanoes condensed to form rain that gradually filled the ocean basins with water. ▼

to form water. This water then made up the world's oceans.

A gradual buildup

Light and heat from the Sun began to break up some of the oceans' water and release oxygen. Oxygen built up in the atmosphere and slowly began forming a layer of ozone. Ozone is a form of oxygen that shields Earth's surface from most of the harmful rays of the Sun. Without this ozone layer, these rays would harm living things. A few forms of plant life evolved in shallow pools, deep enough under water to be safe from the Sun's rays. They began to make their own food, as green plants still do, by a process called photosynthesis.

Photosynthesis also releases oxygen into the atmosphere. So, very slowly, the plants added to Earth's supply of oxygen in the atmosphere.

In time, Earth's atmosphere contained about one-tenth the present amounts of oxygen and ozone. But this was enough to allow plants to survive closer to the surface of the oceans, and microscopic plankton plants still grow there. This happened about 600 million years ago, just before the Cambrian period of Earth's history.

▲ Top: a young, rugged mountain — Machapuchare in Nepal. Bottom: an older mountain, partly worn away — a peak in the Mlange Massif, Malawi.

Life Begins

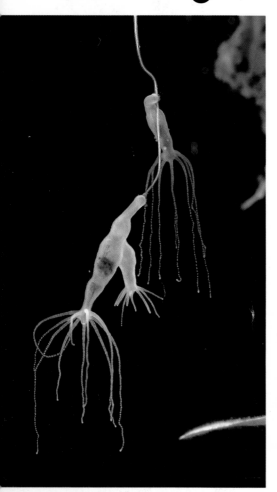

Life could not begin on land because in the early years of Earth there was not enough oxygen in the atmosphere. So it seems certain that life began in the oceans.

For a long time, scientists thought life depended on the heat and light of the Sun that green plants use for photosynthesis. But in the 1970s, they discovered clams, giant worms, and mussels living in one of the deepest parts of the sea, about two miles (3 km) below the ocean surface. The Sun's rays cannot reach such depths.

These animals feed on bacteria that grow in hot water welling up from cracks in the seabed So the energy needed for living comes from inside Earth. It seems likely that the earliest forms of life started in much the same way.

Earliest evidence
Some of the earliest evidence of life comes from Canada and South Africa. There, geologists have found some bun-shaped rocks, called

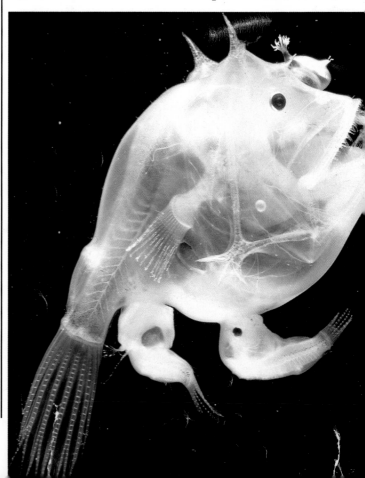

▲ A hydra, a simple freshwater animal whose ancestors probably evolved at the same time that stromatolites formed.

A female deep-sea anglerfish ▶ with two parasitic males. Bony fish evolved less than 150 million years ago.

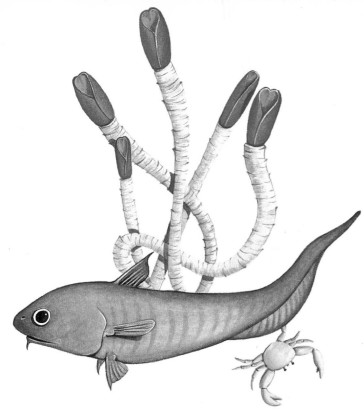

Spontaneous generation

For thousands of years, ever since the days of the ancient Greeks, people believed that life could develop from lifeless matter — for instance, from ground soaked by rain and warmed by sunlight. This process was called spontaneous generation. Scientists now think that life actually began by a chemical process.

◀ Crabs, fish, and giant worms thrive deep in the ocean. They get their food from bacteria that grow in hot water welling up from cracks in the ocean floor.

stromatolites, that are about 3.5 billion years old. Stromatolites result from the action of very simple organisms called cyanobacteria. These bacteria form slimy layers on rocks and wet ground. Similar bacteria have been found in ancient rocks in Minnesota. Bacteria belong to the Monera kingdom.

These and other early forms of life were all simple one-celled organisms. The oldest multi-celled animals discovered so far are some fossils in rocks found in Australia and Newfoundland. These fossils belong to creatures that lived in Precambrian times, over 600 million years ago. They include jellyfish, various kinds of worms, and creatures related to starfish.

Fossilized sea animals that lived long ago. They are all examples of the simple creatures, such as worms and jellyfish, that were among the earliest known ocean dwellers. ▼

Dickinsonia, a worm

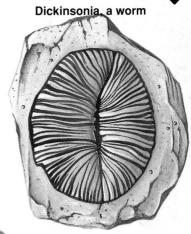

nia, a sea pen

Medusina, a jellyfish

Spriggina, a worm

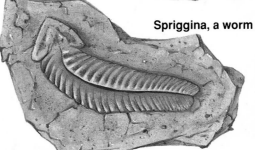

Animals without Backbones

Jellyfish, like this one, live in all the oceans of the world. ▼

The sea scorpion

One of the most terrifying prehistoric marine animals was the giant sea scorpion *Pterygotus*. This extinct relative of modern scorpions was over seven feet (2 m) long. It had six pairs of limbs: a pair of claws, four pairs of legs for walking, and a pair of paddles for swimming.

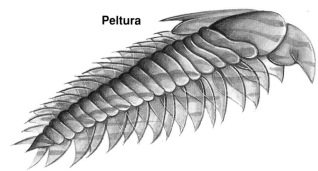

Peltura

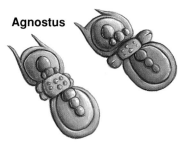

Agnostus

Invertebrates

The time from the late Precambrian period to the beginning of the Devonian period is sometimes called the age of marine, or sea, invertebrates because for most of that time invertebrates were the only animals in the sea. Invertebrates are animals without backbones. Even today there are many times more invertebrates than vertebrates, or animals with backbones.

In Precambrian times, all these marine animals had soft bodies. For this reason, we have few fossil remains, except trace fossils that show where the animals crawled across the seabed or burrowed down into it.

Early in the Cambrian period, animals began to develop hard parts — shells, chalky tubes, and chalky skeletons that were external or outside the animals. These hard parts fossilized readily, and from them we have a much better idea of animal life from Cambrian times to the present.

Trilobites

One of the most common sea animals in this period of Earth's history was the trilobite, a

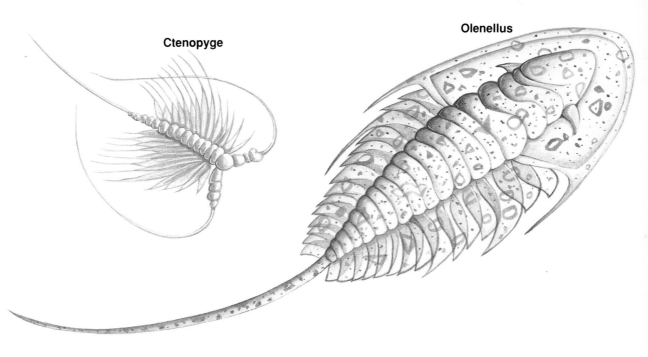

Ctenopyge

Olenellus

small creature with a hard shell. Trilobites belonged to the arthropods, a group that includes present-day spiders, insects, and crustaceans. More than 2,500 trilobite species flourished for about 370 million years.

Mollusks of the past

The sea was also home to many kinds of mollusks. Today's living mollusks include snails, limpets, oysters, and octopuses. Fossil mollusks include animals similar to many present-day species.

Two kinds of mollusk no longer exist, but their fossils are common. Ammonites were mollusks with coiled shells. They lived from the Devonian period to the end of the Cretaceous period. They varied in size from less than one inch (2.5 cm) wide to over six feet (2 m). Their shells were divided into chambers that were filled with air or gas. The only kind of mollusk today that is similar is the nautilus.

Belemnites had bullet-shaped shells, called "devil's thunderbolts" by the people who first found them. Their soft parts were probably like those of today's cuttlefish.

▲ Millions of years ago, many strange-looking invertebrates evolved in the sea.

A Who's Who of Invertebrates

There are over 20 invertebrate phyla. These are the main ones:

- **Sponges**

- **Jellyfish and corals**

- **Comb jellies and sea gooseberries**

- **Mollusks,** such as octopuses, clams, slugs, oysters, and snails

- **Earthworms, leeches, and lugworms**

- **Arthropods:** a mixed group including mites, scorpions, crabs, spiders, insects, shrimp, lobsters, horseshoe crabs, and trilobites

- **Starfish, brittle stars, sea cucumbers, and sea urchins**

Animals with Backbones

The development of backbones was a major step forward in evolution. Animals that have backbones are called vertebrates. They include nearly all the biggest, most active, and intelligent animals. But there are few vertebrate species. For every kind of vertebrate, there are over 25 invertebrate species.

Many invertebrates have their skeletons outside their bodies. Beetles, for example, have a hard outer case. An external skeleton is like a suit of armor — it does not grow along with the animal. Instead, the growing animal has to molt, or shed, its outer casing. It has a new and larger soft case underneath that quickly hardens to become the new exoskeleton.

Vertebrates belong to a larger group called the chordates. Three other groups of chordates live in the sea. They do not have a true backbone, but instead have a primitive supporting rod, called a notochord. They include acorn worms, sea squirts, and lancelets.

A vertebrate has its skeleton inside its body, so it never needs to molt. The skeleton grows along with its body. Most skeletons are made of hard, strong bone. But two groups of fish,

▲ A bony skeleton, that of a gorilla, typical of vertebrates.

A scene showing some of the plants and animals of the Jurassic period. ▶

including lampreys and sharks, have softer, tough cartilage, or gristle, instead of bone.

Hard outer cases

A few vertebrates, such as turtles, armadillos, and some dinosaurs, developed hard bony plates or shells for protection. The main nerves of a vertebrate's body run inside the backbone, or spine. At the head end, the nerves enlarge to form the brain, which is protected by the skull. Another feature of vertebrates is skin that almost entirely covers the body.

Because vertebrates have strong internal skeletons, many have been able to grow much bigger than invertebrates. This is important for land animals because air, unlike water, does not support bodies. The development of the brain enables vertebrates to do more complex things than can invertebrates, which do not have real brains.

We know very little about the evolution of vertebrates. The earliest vertebrate fossils found are of some primitive fish related to modern lampreys and hagfish. These date from Cambrian times, 570 million years ago.

▲ A bull shark, a species that lives in tropical seas.

A Who's Who of Vertebrates

Vertebrates are in seven classes of the phylum Chordata:

- **Lampreys and hagfish:** fish that do not have jaws

- **Sharks and rays:** fish with cartilage instead of bone

- **Bony fish:** all the other important and common fish

- **Frogs, toads, newts, and salamanders:** the amphibians that live both in the water and on the land

- **Reptiles:** crocodiles, lizards, turtles, snakes, and dinosaurs

- **Birds**

- **Mammals:** all the animals that feed their young milk, from mice to whales and elephants

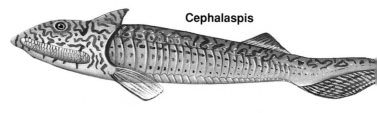

Cephalaspis

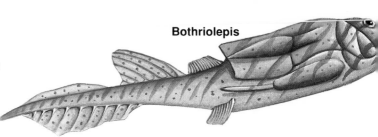

Bothriolepis

Fish

Tricky fossils

Fish give us another example of the need to think carefully about the fossils we find. One group of fossil fish was found with bodies curved instead of flat. At first, people thought that this curved shape suggested that the fish had been poisoned. Then they realized that when dead fish dry, their bodies often contract into a curved shape.

A blue-spotted ray, a typical fish with cartilage.

The first fish swam in the seas some time durin the Cambrian period. They were jawless fish. They were also the first vertebrates, and they had a very simple structure. Because they had cartilage instead of bone, they left few fossils. Two kinds of jawless fish are still living — hagfish and lampreys.

Four classes of fish with jaws appeared in the Silurian and Devonian periods. Two classes — those with thorny skin and those with plated skin — became extinct. The other classes survive to this day. All four groups of fish lived in the Devonian period. This was a time when fish began to dominate the life of the oceans, as they still do to this day.

Fish that have cartilage instead of bone belong to the class Chondrichthyes. Modern fish of this class are the sharks and rays. Unlik

Jamoytius

Lunaspis

◀ Fish of the Silurian and Devonian periods. Cephalaspis and Jamoytius were jawless fish, like modern lampreys. Bothriolepis and Lunaspis were early jawed fish.

other kinds of fish, sharks and rays do not have swim bladders, or gas pouches, to help keep them afloat. Instead, they have plenty of fat that is lighter than water.

Keeping in the swim

A shark keeps afloat by swimming forward. If it stops swimming, it will sink. Sharks can turn and change depth quickly, but they cannot swim backward.

There are more kinds of bony fish than any other vertebrates, in the sea or on the land. There are many thousands of fossil fish, some that are unlike modern fish. However, deep-sea divers are always finding unknown species of fish. So one day we may come across another fish we thought was extinct, like the coelacanth.

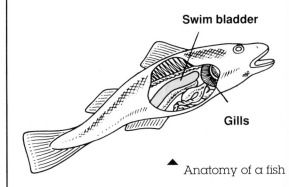

Swim bladder

Gills

▲ Anatomy of a fish

A surgeonfish. This is a bony type that lives among coral reefs. ▼

4: LIFE COMES ASHORE

Land Plants and Animals

Opposite page: Frogs emerged around 200 million years ago. A modern descendant is the red-eyed leaf frog, found on the Caribbean coast of Costa Rica. ▶ ▶

The West African lungfish is a modern relative of the early lungfish that were the first vertebrates to venture onto dry land. This animal spends the hot summer months sheltering in mud. ▼

More than 500 million years ago, plants and water animals began moving from salty seas to freshwater rivers. The first marine, or sea, plants were simple, one-celled organisms. The first large plants we know of grew in swampy areas and peat bogs. These were water plant with their roots under water and their tops in the air. They flourished about 400 million years ago, during the Silurian period.

Within 100 million years, plants had spread from the swamps to cover a large area of the land. As they grew and spread, they released more oxygen into the atmosphere. Life on lan became easier in this oxygen-enriched air.

The first land animals were probably anima with jointed limbs — ancestors of today's insects, spiders, and crustaceans.

Leglike fins

The first vertebrates to venture onto land were lungfish. These fish lived in rivers and fresh-water lakes. Lungfish still exist. Besides using gills to breathe in water, as other fish do, lungfish have lungs for breathing air. Some modern species cannot breathe in water. The fins of lungfish are on fleshy stumps that the fish can use to "walk" on the riverbed or to drag themselves over land.

After the lungfish came the amphibians, which developed in the Devonian period. For more than 100 million years they were the dominant land animals. Some prehistoric amphibians grew up to 13 feet (4 m) long, although others were only about one foot (30 cm) long.

Frogs are modern-day amphibians. They lay their eggs in water, and the young, known as tadpoles, live and breathe in water. As they mature, they grow legs, come onto land, and breathe air.

Many kinds of amphibians are now extinct. But three groups of amphibians still survive: frogs and toads, newts and salamanders, and caecilians, wormlike amphibians without legs.

▲ Labyrinthodonts were early amphibians that looked somewhat like today's salamanders. Many were very large animals. They died out about 190 million years ago.

A Who's Who of Amphibians

Here are the three groups of amphibians living today:

▪ **Frogs and toads** make up the order Anura, which means "tailless." They have long back legs that enable them to jump. The adults do not have tails.

▪ **Newts and salamanders** make up the order Caudata, which means "tailed." These animals have tails as well as legs.

▪ **Caecilians** form the order Apoda, which means "legless." They have no legs and are slim, wormlike creatures that live in the tropics.

Changing

▲ Even a bare wall can provide a habitat for mosses and lichens.

▼ A polar bear roams the Arctic snows. A thick layer of fat under its heavy fur helps it survive, even in temperatures as low as -34°F (-37°C).

Animals moved out of the water and became adapted to life on land. We must understand this in order to realize how prehistoric life evolved from simple to complex forms.

As worms burrow into the ground, their slim, flexible bodies seem the ideal shape for pushing through the soil. Many birds sleep perched in trees. Their legs are constructed so that when the birds relax, their claws grip the branch on which they are perching more tightly. This keeps the birds from falling off while they sleep.

It is easy to think that the worm and the bird have developed in order to burrow and perch. But what really happens in evolution is that a creature develops some quality that fits, or adapts, it for a certain way of life, and it then lives in that way.

A place in the world

Every plant and animal has its place in the world. Ecologists — scientists who study relationships between organisms and where they live — call such places niches. The term "niche" refers not only to the actual place but to such factors as climate and available food.

Some niches are very general. A rabbit, for example, will do well almost anywhere it can find a good supply of grass and other green plants to eat. Other kinds of niches are more

◀ Koalas live in eucalyptus trees in the forests of eastern Australia. They feed on the leaves of the trees and rarely eat other plants.

Two lions, a male and a female, charge through the African grassland. Lions often work in groups to hunt animals such as antelope and zebras, with the female lions doing most of the work. ▼

specialized. A koala feeds only on certain eucalyptus trees, cacti flourish in deserts, and mangrove trees grow only in swampy places.

Scientists have found that differences in species develop most quickly on islands or other isolated places. While in the Galápagos Islands, Charles Darwin noticed that 14 species of finch had evolved. And each finch was able to find and eat a different kind of food.

Scientists think that these finches are descended from a few birds that landed on the islands millions of years ago. The birds that did best in each of the 14 ecological niches were the ones that thrived and left the most descendants.

Tool for a bird

One of the finches Darwin saw, the woodpecker finch, can do something that few birds are able to do. It uses a tool to get its food. The finch has a short, stout beak that it uses to chop its way into the bark of trees to get at insect grubs. But it does not have a long tongue nor a beak slim enough to pull the grubs out of their burrow. So it uses a small twig or a thorn from a cactus to pull the grubs out. Few birds use tools in this way.

Coal Forests

▲ An artist's impression of what the Carboniferous tropical forests probably looked like. Giant ferns, horsetails, and club mosses grew as tall as trees. Their roots were in swamps, just like mangrove trees of today.

Kinds of coal

There are several different kinds of coal. They vary according to how and when they were formed. The most commonly used coal is soft, bituminous coal that breaks into large rectangular blocks. Anthracite is the hardest coal because it was formed deep down at great pressure. Lignite, or brown coal, was formed most recently and at shallower depths.

During the Carboniferous period, much of the land that is now Europe, Asia, and North America was covered by tropical swamps. Lush forests of giant trees grew in these swamps. Most of the trees were quite different from modern forest trees.

Some trees were club mosses. Today, club mosses are just small mosslike plants. But in the Carboniferous period, some club mosses grew into massive trees more than 100 feet (30 m) tall. Giant ferns and horsetails also grew as common trees in those prehistoric forests.

We know about these forests and their plants because their remains have survived as the coal we dig out of the ground and burn.

When plants die in wet places, such as swamps, they rot to form a thick layer of decaying vegetable matter. You might find such a rotted layer near the bottom of a garden compost heap.

Coal formation

In time, this matted layer becomes buried under other layers. The layers compress and heat up to form peat. Peat is the first stage in the formation of coal. There are huge areas of peat in the United States, Canada, Finland, Germany, Britain, Ireland, and the Soviet Union.

In the prehistoric swamps, rising rivers washed over the peat beds and buried them with layers of sand and mud. When the land dried out again, more forests grew, only to decay and form new layers on top of the old. This is why we find coal in seams. Coal seams are layers ranging from a few inches to many feet thick. They are separated by layers of rock that formed from the sand and mud. Fossils of marine plants and animals are sometimes found in the rock layers. This shows that the forests grew close to prehistoric seacoasts, probably in tidal river mouths.

Within coal itself, we sometimes find the fossil remains of bark, seeds, cones, and other plant debris. Fossils of insects and other small creatures also appear.

▲ Tree ferns still grow in tropical lands. These ferns are in a forest in Malaysia.

Peat, an early stage of coal formation, occurs in many parts of the world. Here, people are digging it out to be dried and used as fuel. ▼

Cones and Flowers

Ferns, horsetails, and club mosses made up the Carboniferous forests. All reproduce by means of spores that can be seen on the undersides of present-day fern fronds.

Some tree species of today have been around since Devonian times. They are trees like conifers, such as spruce, larch, or pine trees. Their naked seeds are easy to see in their cones. By the time they are ripe, the seeds have developed little wings. The wind blows them away to land on the ground and start new trees.

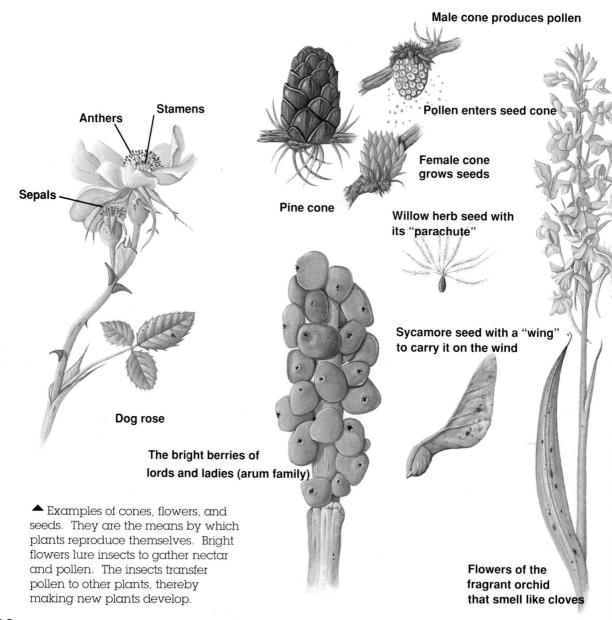

Male cone produces pollen

Pollen enters seed cone

Female cone grows seeds

Pine cone

Anthers

Stamens

Sepals

Dog rose

Willow herb seed with its "parachute"

Sycamore seed with a "wing" to carry it on the wind

The bright berries of lords and ladies (arum family)

Flowers of the fragrant orchid that smell like cloves

▲ Examples of cones, flowers, and seeds. They are the means by which plants reproduce themselves. Bright flowers lure insects to gather nectar and pollen. The insects transfer pollen to other plants, thereby making new plants develop.

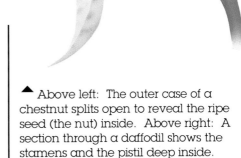

Flowering plants take over

These naked-seed trees formed the world's main forests for about 200 million years. Then, about 140 million years ago, in the Cretaceous period, flowering plants arrived in a botanical "explosion." Their seeds are hidden inside fruit. Within a short time, geologically speaking, flowering plants spread all over Earth. They were very successful in evolutionary terms. We do not know when the first flowering plants evolved, but the earliest known flower fossil, which was found in Colorado, is about 65 million years old.

This plant revolution completely changed the appearance of Earth. It also brought about a major change of food for the animals that were living at that time.

Two groups of animals have evolved in close association with flowering plants. They are insects that carry pollen from one flower to another, and large vegetarian mammals, such as cattle, that depend on grasses and other flowering plants for their food. Although mammals have existed since the Triassic period, they became Earth's dominant animals only after the development of flowering plants. So we see how one form of prehistoric life depended on another.

You can tell how successful flowering plants have been because there are more than 236,000 living species today. By contrast, there are fewer than 4,000 living species of the naked-seed plants.

▲ Above left: The outer case of a chestnut splits open to reveal the ripe seed (the nut) inside. Above right: A section through a daffodil shows the stamens and the pistil deep inside.

▲ Some plants — like this sundew — attract insects in order to eat them. Such plants grow in poor soil, so insects supply needed nutrients.

Rulers of Earth

▲ A duck-billed dinosaur and a small horned dinosaur of the Cretaceous period.

The skeleton of a dinosaur partly reconstructed to show how it fed. ▼

Reptiles, the first true land vertebrates, probab[ly] descended from amphibians. We find the earliest reptile fossils in rocks 300 million years [old]. One big difference between amphibians and reptiles is in the eggs they lay. The eggs [of] most amphibians, like those of other water animals, are soft. With many amphibians, the [ir] eggs must be fertilized in water after they are laid. The eggs of reptiles and birds are enclose[d] in a membrane, or skin. They are fertilized before they are laid. In birds and many reptile[s] the egg has another outer casing, a hard shell[.] The shell and membrane keep the egg from drying out. But they allow the egg to "breathe[."] Oxygen can enter the egg from the air, and carbon dioxide can leave from the inside.

Ancestors of the mammals

The earliest reptiles had shapes something like stocky crocodiles. In the Permian and early Triassic periods, the dominant animals formed a group called the mammal-like reptiles. Som[e] were very small, but others were as large as a rhinoceros. These mammal-like reptiles died out in the Triassic period. They left behind their descendants — the first mammals.

Those early mammals were very small. The real rulers of Earth throughout the Mesozoic era were the reptiles. Two groups took over from the mammal-like reptiles. One group formed the early lizards and their modern descendants, the snakes. These early lizards were mostly insect-eaters.

We call the second group of lizards archosaurs, which means "ancient lizards." The archosaurs lived in rivers and near the seashore. They spent most of their time in the water, hunting for fish, their main food.

Some archosaurs developed a sprawling way of walking. They were the ancestors of present-day crocodiles. Other archosaurs developed long, powerful hind legs and short front legs, like those of modern kangaroos. They were the ancestors of the dinosaurs.

Snakes were the last group of reptiles to evolve. Few of their fossils are found because their skeletons are so fragile. This Californian mountain king snake is lying in the sunshine, warming up so it can go hunting for food. ▼

◀ Like this Nile crocodile, reptiles rest in the shade to keep themselves from overheating when temperatures are high. Crocodiles were well established by about 200 million years ago, and their shape has hardly changed. ▼

The Dinosaurs

Bird-hipped dinosaurs

There were many extraordinary shapes among the bird-hipped dinosaurs. Some had hard plates and spines on their backs that protected them against the meat-eaters. Stegosaurus had plates that might have stood up like a fish's fins. Triceratops and some others had horns like those of a rhinoceros.

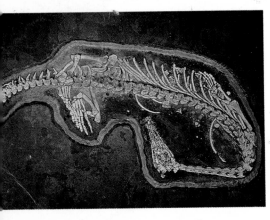

▲ The fossil skeleton from Brazil of Mesosaurus, a small dinosaur that lived part of the time in the water.

Some of the many kinds of dinosaurs that flourished in the age of reptiles. Slender-winged pterosaurs fly overhead. ▶ ▶

At the beginning of the Triassic period, all the world's land area was in one huge supercontinent called Pangaea. The climate was generally warm and moist. Dinosaurs lived in every area and ruled life on Earth for 140 million years. During this time, Pangaea slowly split into two parts, Gondwanaland in the south and Laurasia in the north. Both parts continued to break into smaller continents.

The dinosaurs developed all kinds of shapes and sizes. The smallest of these reptiles were about the size of a present-day chicken. But many dinosaurs were quite large.

The largest we know of was Ultrasaurus. It was the biggest animal that ever lived on land, and was 115 feet (35 m) long from nose tip to tail tip. With its long neck, it was tall enough to look over a modern three-story house.

Giant vegetarians

There were two basic kinds of dinosaurs. We can tell them apart by the shape of their hipbones. One group had hips like modern lizards. The other group had birdlike hips.

The lizard-hipped dinosaurs included both meat-eaters and plant-eaters. Some, such as Diplodocus and Brachiosaurus, were huge, slow-moving plant-eaters that walked on all fours. The meat-eaters, including the fierce *Tyrannosaurus rex*, walked on their hind legs. They had long teeth and sharp claws that they used to tear their prey.

Some bird-hipped dinosaurs, such as Iguanodon, walked on their hind legs, like their lizard-hipped cousins. They included the hadrosaurs, which had bills like that of a duck. Each animal's bill had up to 2,000 teeth in it!

Modern reptiles are cold-blooded — their blood is at nearly the same temperature as the air around them. They have to warm up in the Sun, or cool off in the shade or in water. Mammals and birds, which are warm-blooded, have a steady body heat. Fur or feathers keep their heat in. Some scientists think that dinosaurs might have been warm-blooded.

Rhamphorhynchus

Apatosaurus

Tyrannosaurus rex

Lesothosaurus

Compsognathus

nychus

Prolercerta

David Holmes

Swimming and Flying Reptiles

An ichthyosaur leaps and dives ▶ after fish, while a long-necked plesiosaur swims under water. In the sky, a flock of Pteranodon — large pterosaurs with wingspans of 16 feet (5 m) — glide and dive in a hunt for fish.

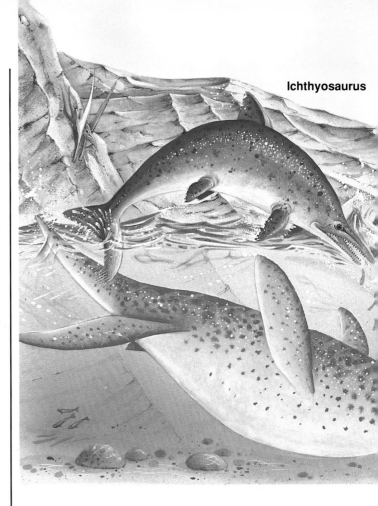

Ichthyosaurus

▲ Turtles have existed for about 200 million years. Even the earliest known fossils had complete upper and lower shells like those of modern turtles, such as this Atlantic logger-head turtle.

Some dinosaurs paddled in swampy areas. Crocodiles swam in rivers and shallow seas, just as their modern descendants do. But some prehistoric reptiles swam in the oceans, as whales and porpoises do today. There were two kinds of these marine reptiles: ichthyosaurs which means "fish-lizards," and plesiosaurs, which means "near-lizards."

The "winged lizards"
While ichthyosaurs and plesiosaurs took to the sea, other reptiles took to the air. We call them pterosaurs, which means "winged lizards," or pterodactyls, meaning "winged fingers."

The first reptiles to take to the air were gliders like the flying squirrels of today. They lived in trees and "parachuted" from one tree to another or to the ground. They lived in the Triassic period. The "parachute" was formed by two pairs of skin folds. One pair linked the elbows

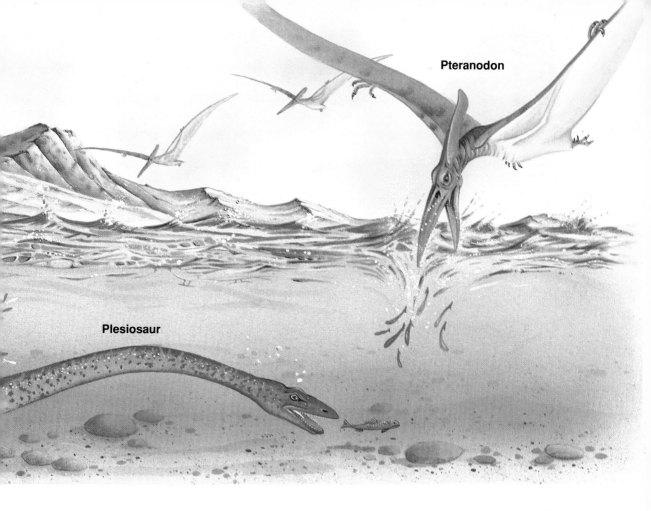

Pteranodon

Plesiosaur

and knees; the other folds ran from the ankles to partway down the long tail.

The true pterosaurs had wings of skin similar to those of modern bats. In 1971, the fossilized skeleton of one pterosaur was found in the Soviet Union, complete with its skin, which was hairy. Scientists think the pterosaurs were warm-blooded animals. Early pterosaurs had long tails and teeth in their beaks. Later ones did not have these features.

The smallest pterosaurs were about the size of a sparrow. The largest pterosaur known was Quetzalcoatlus, a vulturelike reptile with a wingspan of up to 57 feet (16 m). That is about five times the wingspan of the wandering albatross, the bird with the biggest wingspan today. Pteranodon was another huge pterosaur. Its wingspan was 25 feet (7.5 m). Pteranodon had no tail, but its head had a long bony crest on the back for balance.

Did You Know?

The ichthyosaurs had bodies that were streamlined like those of dolphins, and they paddled their way through the water. They had long jaws and plenty of teeth. They probably gave birth to live young in the water, just as whales do.

Plesiosaurs had barrel-shaped bodies, and they swam through the water with a flying motion, somewhat like penguins. One group of plesiosaurs had very long necks and small heads with sharp teeth. They fed on fish. Another group had short necks and large heads with blunt teeth. They, like the ichthyosaurs, also ate fish and shellfish. At least some of the plesiosaurs seem to have been able to move on land.

Extinction

Natural disasters might have ▶ caused the mass extinctions that occurred in the Cretaceous period. But another reason for animals becoming extinct is that they are no longer suited to the conditions in which they are living.

At the end of the Cretaceous period, after 140 million years of ruling Earth, the dinosaurs die out in what we call a mass extinction. There are no dinosaur fossils after 65 million years ag

A great many other species died out at the same time, including the flying and swimming reptiles — the pterosaurs, the ichthyosaurs, an the plesiosaurs. The ammonites also vanished Yet many kinds of animals still survived, including amphibians, birds, corals, crocodile mammals, snakes, and turtles.

The impact theory
Many scientists think that a body from outer space — a meteoroid, an asteroid, or a comet

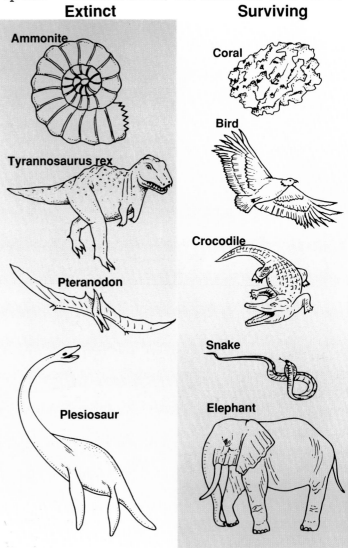

Extinct

Ammonite

Tyrannosaurus rex

Pteranodon

Plesiosaur

Surviving

Coral

Bird

Crocodile

Snake

Elephant

The huge cloud of ash and debris that rose from Mount Saint Helens, Washington, in May 1980 produced darkness over a wide area. But it was a tiny disaster compared with the eruption of Mount Tambora, Indonesia, in 1816. Its dust clogged the world's skies for a whole year.

Killed by plants?

Another possible cause of the end of the dinosaurs was the development of flowering plants. Some people think that the dinosaurs were used to eating other kinds of plants and could not digest the flowering plants, just as giant pandas eat only bamboo shoots.

struck Earth near the end of the Cretaceous period. The impact would have sent massive amounts of debris into the atmosphere to circulate for years. The dust would have blocked sunlight from Earth's surface, causing world temperatures to fall and many species — especially plants — to die out. Proof of this theory is seen in a material called iridium that is rare in Earth's crust but more plentiful in meteorites. Rocks 65 million years old have about as much iridium as meteorites have.

Other theories

Other scientists think that a change in climate could have resulted from any one of several factors right on Earth: large-scale volcanic activity, the sudden rise of mountain ranges, falling sea level, or continents drifting into temperate, or colder, areas of the Earth. Dinosaurs did live later in the tropics than in what are now the temperate parts of Earth. Any flowering plants growing in the temperate areas would die back in winter, leaving little food for the huge animals for months at a time.

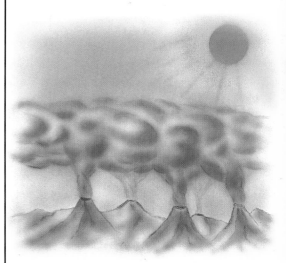

Widespread volcanic activity could have changed Earth's climate. Volcanic dust in the atmosphere would have blocked sunlight from Earth for many years.

6: BIRDS AND MAMMALS

Birds

▲ An artist's impression of what Archaeopteryx probably looked like. No one knows its coloring.

The Fish Bird

Ichthyornis, the Fish Bird, was only about eight inches (20 cm) tall. Its fossils come from the same area as those of Hesperornis. It probably had no teeth. In shape and habits, it was like modern gulls and terns.

Archaeopteryx may have climbed trees in order to take off, like this starling flying from its nest. ▶

Birds descended directly from reptiles. We are lucky enough to have five fossils of what may well have been the very first bird. They were found in Germany. This ancestral bird is called Archaeopteryx, which means "ancient wing."

Archaeopteryx was about the size of a pigeon. It had feathers like a modern bird, but it had heavy bones like a reptile. It was almost certainly too heavy to fly, but it may have climbed trees and glided. It had teeth. Its ancestor was probably not one of the flying reptiles, but Compsognathus, a reptile the size of a modern chicken. Like Compsognathus, Archaeopteryx probably sprinted along the ground to catch the insects and other small animals that it lived on.

We have few fossils of birds from later period But they show that within three million years o Archaeopteryx, all the features of birds as we know them had evolved. These features inclu lightweight, hollow bones, toothless beaks, an a big breastbone that supports the wing muscl

The Dawn Bird

Many of the early birds had teeth. Among them was Hesperornis, the Dawn Bird, a flightless water bird whose fossils have been found in the Great Plains of North America. Hesperornis was shaped like a modern diving bird. Some of these birds were about six feet (2 m) long. They probably caught fish with their teeth.

Even today, birds have many features that are like those of reptiles. The most obvious is the scales, found on the legs of chickens and other birds. These are similar to the scales found on reptiles.

In the past there existed many different types of birds that are no longer around today. ▼

Diatryma

Ichthyornis

Hesperornis

Archaeopteryx

Mammals

▲ This is an artist's impression of an early mammal. We do not really know how many of them would have appeared.

Did You Know?

Mammals now number more than 4,200 species. As with the reptiles, some mammals eat meat, some eat only plants, and some eat both meat and plants.

After the dinosaurs died out, birds and mammals dominated Earth. A mammal is an animal that gives birth to live young and feeds them on their mother's milk. Early mammals fed at night, partly because the much bigger dinosaurs foraged for food during the day.

The first mammals appeared in the Triassic period. They were small, shrewlike animals.

Many of the early mammals that appeared were marsupials. These are animals with pouches like a modern kangaroo. Marsupials give birth to young that are not fully formed. The young climb into the mother's pouch to finish developing. The other mammals, called placental mammals, give birth to young that are fully developed.

The isolated marsupials

The placental mammals became the more dominant of the two types of mammals. This may have been because their more complex brains enabled them to compete better in their different environments. The marsupials survived only in Australia and South America, where they were cut off from their rivals, the placental mammals.

After the extinction of the dinosaurs about 65 million years ago, the mammals began to move into new regions. Many species evolved that have since become extinct, such as the mammoth and the great cave bear.

A number of mammals have taken to life in the seas. They include whales, dolphins, and porpoises, which never come to live on land, and seals and their relatives, which give birth to their young on land. The earliest known whale fossils are about 50 million years old, and the oldest seal fossils date back about 20 million years.

A Who's Who of Mammals

Here are 18 orders of mammals:

- **Egg-laying mammals**, such as the platypus

- **Marsupials**, the pouched mammals, such as kangaroos

- **Insect-eaters**, such as moles

- **Flying lemurs**, which glide rather than fly

- **Bats**, the only mammals that truly fly

- **Primates** — apes and humans

- **Sloths and anteaters**

- **Pangolins**

- **Hares and rabbits**

- **Rodents**, the gnawing animals, such as rats and mice

- **Dolphins, whales and porpoises**, the sea mammals

- **Carnivores**, the meat-eaters, such as cats, bears, and wolves

- **The aardvark**

- **Elephants**

- **Hyraxes**

- **Sea cows**

- **Odd-toed hoofed animals**, such as horses and tapirs

- **Even-toed hoofed animals**, such as pigs, sheep, and cattle

◀ A woolly mammoth. Complete bodies have been found frozen in Siberia, perfectly preserved. The last mammoths died out about 10,000 years ago.

Moving Continents

The continents have not always been where th are now. During the Triassic period, they were joined together to form the supercontinent calle Pangaea, consisting of nearly all the land surfo

During the Jurassic period, Pangaea began to break apart. Over millions of years, the Atlantic Ocean opened up. North America and Europe moved apart, and so did South America and Africa. To the south, Australia, Antarctica, and the Indian subcontinent broke away from Africa. We call this movement of the land continental drift.

Continental drift had an enormous effect on prehistoric life. Pangaea lay much farther

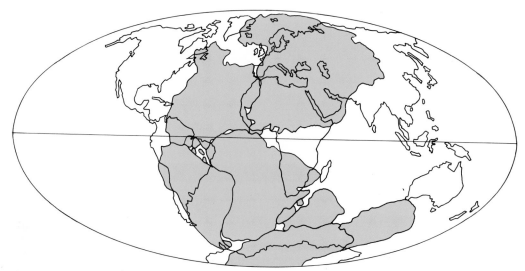

This map shows the continents and how they fitted together to form the supercontinent Pangaea. See the maps on page 6.

Drifting dinosaurs

Dinosaur fossils show the effect of continental drift. At the end of the Jurassic period, the plated dinosaur Stegosaurus died out everywhere except in India, where it lived on for another 50 million years or so. During this time, India was drifting by itself toward Asia, where eventually it collided. The collision forced up the great Himalayan mountain range.

south than most of the land does today. The climate over most of Pangaea was warmer and more even than today's world climate. The dinosaurs thrived in this environment. As Pangaea gradually broke into smaller continents, the climate grew colder. For many plants and animals, it was difficult to adapt to the new conditions.

Animals in isolation

One important result of continental drift was that a number of plant and animal communitie became isolated. Australia had marsupial mammals, but no placental mammals, when it became isolated.

Duckbill platypus

Tasmanian wolf

Kangaroo

As a result, the marsupials developed to fill all the ecological niches that were occupied by the placental mammals in other places. So it had marsupial mice and cats, kangaroos instead of deer or antelope, and Tasmanian wolves instead of gray wolves. Primitive egg-laying mammals, like the duckbill platypus and the echidna, also lived on in Australia and nearby New Guinea.

South America was another island. It was not linked to North America until just over two million years ago. It, too, had marsupials, as well as a number of placental mammals such as the giant ground sloth, which has since died out. One group of South American marsupials, the opossums, still survives and has spread to North America.

▲ Marsupials, such as the kangaroo and the opossum, are descended from ancient stock that survived in the isolated continents of Australia and South America. The two species of sloths that exist today in South America are all that remain of a large group that included the megatheres, giant ground sloths.

Humans Arrive

The figures from left to right show the development of hominids, from the apelike *Australopithecus* to modern *Homo sapiens*. ▼

When Charles Darwin first published *On the Origin of Species* in 1859, many people thought he was claiming that humans were descended from monkeys. But Darwin did not say this.

Three things distinguish hominids from apes. Hominids walk upright, use tools, and communicate with one another by means of language. Fossil skulls can sometimes show whether their owners could speak or merely grunt. The shape of the leg bones shows if they walked upright. The earliest hominid fossil found so far was discovered in 1985 in Kenya. It is about four million years old. It belonged to *Australopithecus*, meaning "Southern Ape." The earliest fossils belong to the species *Australopithecus afarensis*. Three other species of *Australopithecus* have been discovered in southern and eastern Africa: *A. africanus*, which lived about three million years ago, and *A. robustus* and *A. boisei*, which lived

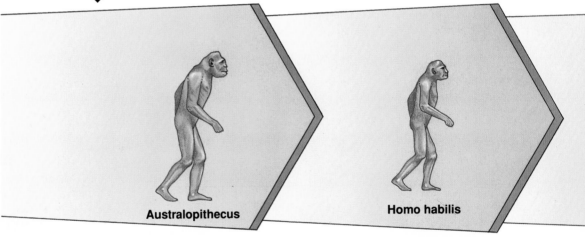

Australopithecus

Homo habilis

A comparison of the skull of modern *Homo sapiens* ("Wise Man") with those of other hominids. The skull of Neanderthal Man looks very similar to that of modern humans. This is because Neanderthal Man was a subspecies of *Homo sapiens* whose scientific name is *Homo sapiens neanderthalensis*. The word "Man" with a capital "M" is used here to indicate a species, including both sexes.

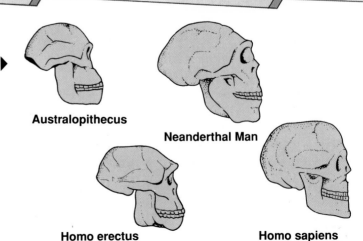

Australopithecus

Neanderthal Man

Homo erectus

Homo sapiens

wo million years ago and may have made imple stone tools.

Humans belong to the genus *Homo*, which neans "Man." The earliest human was *Homo habilis* ("Handy Man"), who lived in East Africa about 1,800,000 years ago, at the same time as *Australopithecus boisei*.

Fossils of *Homo erectus* ("Upright Man") have been found all over the world. The first specimens found came from Indonesia and China. At first, they were called "Java Man" and "Peking Man." Upright Man made better stone tools and used fire. This early human roamed Earth for 1,200,000 years.

Finally, about 300,000 years ago, Upright Man died out and was replaced by *Homo sapiens* — "Wise Man." A strong, rugged form of Wise Man, called Neanderthal Man, lived in Europe during the Ice Age, from about 100,000 to 40,000 years ago. Then he died out.

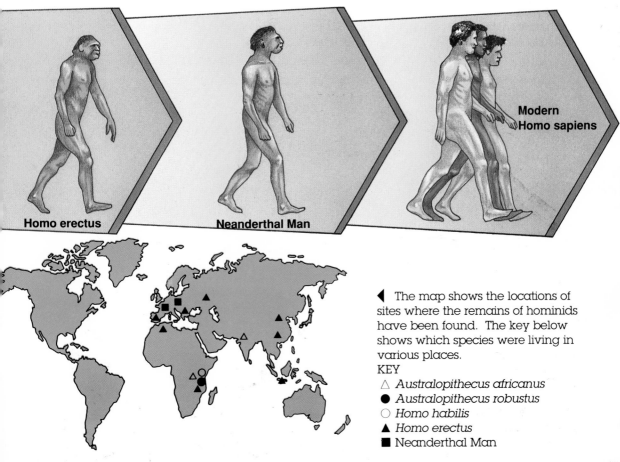

Homo erectus

Neanderthal Man

Modern Homo sapiens

◀ The map shows the locations of sites where the remains of hominids have been found. The key below shows which species were living in various places.

KEY
△ *Australopithecus africanus*
● *Australopithecus robustus*
○ *Homo habilis*
▲ *Homo erectus*
■ Neanderthal Man

The Future

The Galápagos Islands in the Pacific Ocean form a unique habitat, providing ecological niches for species not found elsewhere. They include the Galápagos fur seals and the swallow-tailed gulls seen here. ▼

The study of prehistoric life shows us three things. First, humans evolved very recently in terms of geological time — the whole period of Earth history. Second, the changes we call evolution take place extremely slowly, as far as our own idea of time is concerned. And third, evolution is still going on.

In an incredibly short time, geologically speaking, humans have come to dominate Earth. We have a much bigger effect on our world than even the dinosaurs had. We humans change the landscape wherever we go. We are cutting down tropical forests at an ever-increasing rate, and already half the world's tropical forests are now gone. In doing this, we are destroying the ecological niches where millions of insects and other animals live. If we are not careful, we might cause a catastrophe as great as the two biggest mass extinctions. A nuclear disaster like the one that took place in 1986 at Chernobyl, in the Soviet Union, could also cause worldwide damage to all life on our Earth.

◀ Many plants are rare, such as this Chinese slipper orchid. Fortunately, people are now aware of this, and today, efforts are made to preserve such plants, and in many cases, their habitats as well.

This forest in Celebes, Indonesia, is being cleared for human settlement, with the resulting loss of plants and animals. ▼

Genetic engineering

For some time, plant and animal breeders have improved species for farmers. Now scientists can alter an organism's cells by a process called genetic engineering. This is likely to produce even greater changes in plant and animal life.

Our own future development may change if people establish colonies on the Moon or other planets. Research in Hawaii and the Galápagos Islands shows that new species develop most rapidly in island communities. Colonies on other planets would be island communities on a large scale. Perhaps in a few million years there might be a new species of human!

We learn more every year about how plants and animals have evolved in the past. In time, we may even find out how life itself began.

The Ages of Earth

ERAS	PERIODS	EPOCHS	MILLIONS OF YEARS AGO (at start)
PRECAMBRIAN (Before the Cambrian)		The longest era, about seven times as long as the rest put together. Most of the world's iron ore was deposited. The atmosphere had little oxygen. Some types of algae and soft-bodied forms much like modern jellyfish, sea pens, and sea worms lived in shallow seas.	4,600 (4.6 billion)
PALEOZOIC ("Ancient Life")	**CAMBRIAN**	The earliest period of the Paleozoic era. Most land was together in the supercontinent Gondwanaland. Oxygen increased in the atmosphere. Large trilobites, brachiopods, early sponges, corals, and jawless fish with bony armor appeared in the seas.	570
	ORDOVICIAN	The second period of the Paleozoic era. Sea flooding of all the continents was at its greatest. Abundant sea life included corals, moss animals, shellfish, starfish, and nautiloids.	500
	SILURIAN	The third period of the Paleozoic era. All the continents were flooded with shallow seas. Eurypterids, or sea scorpions, were common. Fish with jaws became abundant in lakes and rivers. The first land plants, psilophytes, probably lived in wet places along the shore.	435
	DEVONIAN	The fourth period of the Paleozoic era, often called the Age of Fish. Large petroleum deposits were made. Fish dominated sea life. Lungfish appeared. Amphibians and insects appeared on land. Early plants grew on land and later became the first large forests.	400
	CARBONIFEROUS	The fifth period of the Paleozoic era. All land formed the supercontinent Pangaea. Forests of giant ferns, horsetails, and conifers grew and later formed most of the world's coal. Insects and vertebrates spread out. Reptiles first appeared. Large sharks ruled the seas.	345
	PERMIAN	The most recent period of the Paleozoic era. The climate became cooler and drier. Amphibians, reptiles, and mammal-like reptiles lived on land. Up to one-half the invertebrate sea species died out near the end of this period. Conifers dominated the land plants.	280

Earth's long history is divided into four main lengths of geological time, called eras. Each era is divided into periods, and the two most recent periods are divided into epochs. They are all shown on this chart.

ERAS	PERIODS	EPOCHS		MILLIONS OF YEARS AGO (at start)
MESOZOIC ("Middle Life")	TRIASSIC	The first period of the Mesozoic era. In the late Triassic, Pangaea began to split into today's continents. The world's climate grew drier. Large reptiles, including the early crocodiles, prospered. Dinosaurs, pterosaurs, and ichthyosaurs evolved. The first mammals, which were small, appeared.		230
	JURASSIC	The second period of the Mesozoic era. Continents had formed but were still connected. The climate was moist and warm. Dinosaurs ruled the Earth. Mammal-like reptiles died out. The earliest known bird, Archaeopteryx, lived near the end of this period. Crocodiles and turtles appeared.		195
	CRETACEOUS	The last period of the Mesozoic era. Half the Earth's land surface was under shallow seas. The Andes rose, and the Alps, the Himalayas, and the Rocky Mountains began rising. The climate was generally mild. Dinosaurs still ruled. Flowering plants appeared. The mass extinction of all dinosaurs ends this period.		140
CENOZOIC ("Recent Life")	TERTIARY	Paleocene	Much more of the world's petroleum was deposited. Extensive volcanic activity took place. The climate cooled rapidly. The continents were in their present places. The Tertiary is the Age of Mammals. Carnivores, rodents, hoofed animals, and primates evolved. An Ice Age took place in the Pleistocene epoch. Later, modern climate zones were established. Modern humans appeared. Large mammals, such as mammoths, ground sloths, and saber-toothed tigers, became extinct.	65
		Eocene		54
		Oligocene		38
		Miocene		26
		Pliocene		12
	QUATERNARY	Pleistocene		2.5
		Recent (Holocene)		0.01

Glossary

Algae (*singular*: alga): Simple organisms that live in seawater and fresh water. Many are made up of just one cell.

Amber: Fossilized resin from conifers that grew millions of years ago, sometimes containing fossilized insects or plants.

Amphibian: Any member of the class Amphibia — vertebrates that usually begin life in the water with gills and later develop lungs. Amphibians include frogs, toads, newts, and salamanders.

Angiosperm: Any of the flowering plants, which have their seeds encased in fruits or shells.

Arthropod: Any member of a phylum of invertebrates that includes insects, spiders, crustaceans, centipedes, and millipedes.

Bacteria (*singular*: bacterium): Simple one-celled organisms; a few can cause diseases.

Cartilage: Gristle, a rubbery structural tissue found in the bodies of vertebrates.

Chemical element: Any of the basic substances from which everything is made.

Class: A rank of living things that comes between phylum (or division) and order.

Conifer: A type of tree that has cones; these trees are usually evergreen.

Continental drift: The movement of continents over the surface of the Earth that has been going on for over 500 million years.

Cyanobacteria: Bacteria that live in the sea and form slimy layers cementing sand to form stromatolites. Cyanobacteria were once known as blue-green algae.

Division: The equivalent for plants of a phylum.

Ecological niche: The place or set of conditions in which an organism lives.

Ecologist: A scientist who studies the relationship between living things and their environment.

Epoch: A division of geological time. A period is divided into epochs.

Era: One of the major divisions of geological time. An era is divided into periods.

Erosion: The wearing away of the Earth's surface by wind, water, gravity, heat and cold, and other natural forces.

Evolution: The process of change in living things that over a long time produces new species.

Extinct: Having died out; no longer existing.

Family: A rank of living things that comes between order and genus.

Fertilize: To make something fertile, or able to reproduce or develop.

Fossil: The remains of an organism that have been preserved, usually in rock.

Gene: The part of a cell that determines heredity, or what characteristics a plant or animal inherits from its parents.

Genetic engineering: The way in which scientists can alter an organism's genes.

Genetics: The study of genes and heredity.

Genus: A rank of living things that comes between family and species.

Geological time: Time as related to the history of Earth.

Geology: The study of the structure and history of the Earth.

Gondwanaland: A prehistoric supercontinent that consisted of the continental masses of present-day South America, Africa, Arabia, Madagascar, India, Australia, Antarctica, and part of China. Gondwanaland existed through the entire Paleozoic era (570 million-230 million years ago). Then it joined Laurasia to form the world continent of Pangaea.

Gymnosperm: A plant, such as a conifer, that does not have its seed inside fruit.

Heredity: The process by which a plant or animal inherits characteristics from its parents; also, the characteristics so inherited.

Hominid: Any humanlike creature, including any prehistoric or modern human.

Igneous rock: Any rock formed from the cooling of molten material from inside the Earth.

Invertebrate: Any animal without a backbone.

Kingdom: The largest group of life forms. There is one kingdom for plants, one for animals, and three for other life forms, such as fungi, bacteria, and amoebas.

Laurasia: A prehistoric supercontinent that consisted of the continental masses of present-day North America, Europe, and Siberia that united near the close of the Paleozoic era (about 230 million years ago), and then joined Gondwanaland to form the world continent of Pangaea.

Mammal: Any vertebrate animal whose offspring are fed by the mother's milk from her mammary glands (teats).

Marsupial: Any mammal that carries its newborn young in a marsupium, or pouch, where it nurses until it completes its development.

Mass extinction: The dying out at the same time of a large number of species.

Membrane: A thin layer of tissue in a plant or an animal.

Metamorphic rock: Any rock that has been changed by heat or pressure, or both, inside the Earth.

Meteorite: A lump of stone or metal that falls from outer space to Earth.

Mold fossil: A hollow in rock that takes the shape of the remains of a living thing that have decayed.

Mollusk: Any member of a phylum of invertebrates that includes clams, octopuses, oysters, slugs, and snails.

Molten: Made liquid by heat; melted.

Natural selection: The evolutionary theory based on the survival of the fittest.

Order: A rank of living things that comes between class and family.

Ozone: A form of oxygen.

Pangaea: The immense prehistoric world continent into which all of Earth's present continental masses were combined during the Permian and Triassic periods.

Period: A major division of geological time. Eras are divided into periods.

Photosynthesis: The process by which green plants, algae, and some bacteria can make substances, such as sugars, from water and carbon dioxide with the aid of sunlight.

Phylum: A rank of animals or other living things between kingdom and class. Botanists use the term *division* to describe a similar rank of plants.

Placental mammal: Any mammal in which the young before birth are nourished inside the mother's body through a temporary blood-rich organ called a placenta.

Plankton: The mass of tiny animals and plants that drift close to the surface of the sea.

Protective coloration: Warning colors, such as black and yellow, that suggest to a predator that an animal is harmful or not good to eat.

Radioactivity: The emission of waves and particles of energy from certain substances, such as uranium or radium, as a result of nuclear reactions.

Sedimentary rock: Any rock, such as sandstone or limestone, formed by the deposition of small particles as sediment in water.

Species: The rank of living things below genus; organisms of the same species are alike to the point where they can produce offspring.

Spontaneous generation: An erroneous theory that living things could originate from non-living matter.

Stony fossil: Any fossil that is formed in or of rock.

Strata (*singular:* stratum): The layers formed by rock in the Earth's crust.

Stromatolites: Fossil rocks formed by layers of cyanobacteria.

Tectonic plates: Large areas of the Earth's crust on which continents and oceans rest.

Temperate: Neither too hot nor too cold.

Trace fossil: A fossil track, hole, or other mark left by the activity of a living thing.

Tropics: Hot regions near the Earth's equator.

Ungulate: Any mammal with hoofs.

Vertebrate: Any animal with a backbone.

Index

A **boldface** number shows that the entry is illustrated on that page. The same page often has text about the entry, too.